GROW YOUR OWN VEGETABLES:

3 Book Bundle

Book 1: The Vegetable Growers Guide to Companion Planting: The Role of Flowers, Herbs & Organic Thinking

Book 2. Raised Bed Gardening Planting Guide: Growing Vegetables The Easy Way.

Book 3. Vegetable Container Gardening: Growing Vegetables In Containers & Planters.

By

James Paris

Published By www.deanburnpublications.com

Blog: www.planterspost.com

Relevant Books by Same Author

Raised Bed Gardening 5 Book Bundle

Raised Bed Gardening 3 Book Bundle

Companion Planting

Growing Berries

Square Foot Gardening

Square Foot Vs Raised Bed Gardening

Vegetable Gardening Basics

Copyright:

Copyright 2014, James Paris

All rights reserved. Copyright protected. Duplicating, reprinting or distributing this material in any form whatsoever without the express written consent of the author is prohibited.

While reasonable attempts have been made to assure the accuracy of the information contained within this publication, the author does not assume any responsibility for errors, omissions or contrary interpretation of this information, and any damages incurred by that.

The author and publisher shall have neither liability nor responsibility to any person or entity with respect to any loss or damage caused or alleged to be caused either directly or indirectly by any information presented in this work

Table of Contents

Book 1 - The Vegetable Growers Guide to Companion Planting: 6

Introduction to Companion Planting Vegetables: 7

The History of Companion Planting: 10

5 Good Reasons For Companion Planting: 12

The influence of Allelopathy: 16

Why Plants Grow Well Together: 19

Plants That Grow Well Together: 22

Plants That Do Not Grow Well Together: 30

Beneficial Herbs: 32

Top 5 Benefits of Raised Bed Gardening: 36

Top 5 Benefits of Container Gardening: 42

Creating Organic Compost: 47

Book 2: 54

Raised Bed Gardening Planting Guide – Growing Vegetables The Easy Way 54

Introduction to Raised Bed Gardening 55

   Advantages of a raised bed garden 57

Building A Raised Bed Garden 59

Building a timber raised bed 61

Building a raised bed from brick 65

Dry stone raised bed 68

Other raised bed examples 70

Filling and Modifications **72**

Working Tips For A Raised Bed **80**

Vegetables For A Raised Bed **82**

Book 3: **86**

Vegetable Container Gardening Growing Vegetables In Containers & Planters **86**

Chapter 1: Planting – Where Am I Coming From ? **87**

Chapter 2: Time Rolls On **91**

Chapter 3: Planter Types and Ideas **94**

Chapter 4: Container Planting Top Tips.................... **105**

Chapter 5: Matching Planter to Plant **115**

Thanks From The Author **120**

Book 1 - The Vegetable Growers Guide to <u>Companion Planting:</u>

The Role of Flowers Herbs & Organic Thinking

By

James Paris

Published By

www.deanburnpublications.com

Blog: www.planterspost.com

Introduction to Companion Planting Vegetables:

Some individuals may consider companion planting to be some kind of 'New Age' holistic fad; however as the good book says 'There is nothing new under the sun.'
 Although the whole aspect of companion planting seems finally to have gathered some recognition; the fact is that it has been practiced for centuries – ever since man first picked up a shovel and decided to grow his own food, rather than (or as well as), chase it around with a bow and arrow!

In fact companion planting could be seen as the very foundation stone upon which the whole organic or green movement is built; the reason for this is simple. If done properly, companion planting does away with the need for chemical fertilisers and bug sprays; produces the best, healthy crops; and is the most environmentally friendly way to produce your own fresh food as a consequence.

Not only can you save money by 'going green,' but by making use of the companion planting methods described in this book, you – and your children – can live healthier lives by cutting out the chemical fertilizers and pesticides, that are inevitably included in the daily diet of those individuals who couldn't care less about what they consume, or indeed how it has been grown.

So what is Companion Planting?
Companion planting is simply a form of polyculture, and when used intelligently along with gardening techniques such as Raised Bed Gardening, or Container Gardening for instance; then this method of sharing the mutual benefits of the individual plants, is capable of producing fantastic results. In fact, companion planting is likened to putting together the perfect partnership; creating results in respect of larger, healthier crops that the individual plants could not produce.

The fact is that, just like we homo-sapiens; plants need good companions to thrive and flourish in their environment. Unlike us however, being rooted to the spot, they cannot choose their friends – we have to choose friends or companions for them! How do we choose friends that they will like, and get along with? Simple really. We take into account the strong points and needs of the individual plants, and then put them together – in fact the gardener takes on the role of match-maker!

I'll bet you never considered running a dating agency for vegetables before this – did you? Joking apart; the fact is that if the plants thrive – alongside the ideal companions that you have provided - then the harvest is bountiful – and everyone is happy.

The History of Companion Planting:

As was alluded to in the introduction, companion planting is nothing new; and in fact is fairly well documented. The Chinese for instance, have been using this method to protect and promote their rice crops for over 1,000 years.

By planting the mosquito fern as a companion for their rice crops, that hosts a special cyanobacterium that fixes nitrogen from the atmosphere. It also helps to block out the light so that competing weeds cannot prosper; the rice being planted only when it is tall enough to stick above the fern.

The native Indians of North America are widely accredited for pioneering the 'Three Sisters' technique of planting corn, beans and squash together. The corn would act as a trellis for the beans, which in turn laid down nitrogen that benefited the corn and the squash. Sunflowers could also be grown, usually a short distance away from the three sisters to act help draw away aphids.

Companion planting in fact, although ancient in origin, has grown up alongside the whole Organic Farming movement. With the emphasis on healthier foods, organically grown; this holistic approach to growing vegetables has taken on a whole new importance for the modern, environmentally aware grower.

5 Good Reasons For Companion Planting:

There are many reasons that can be cited to promote the idea of companion planting, from environmental to personal. Here are just five of the most powerful reasons in my opinion.

1. Environmental:
Protecting the environment is a hugely important issue these days, and rightly so. If more people got themselves involved with the principles behind organic and companion gardening, then we would not be polluting both our bodies and the land, with chemical fertilizers or poisonous insecticides to the extent that we are.
This does not just involve ourselves, but has ramifications for generations to come.

Millions of tons of waste go into landfills every year, which in fact could easily be recycled – to our own benefit! Composting as a part of growing your own vegetables and becoming more environmentally aware, is one way to help balance this wastage.

It can be correctly stated that companion planting, when done in concert with other organic growing methods is good for our bodies and good for the environment – a win-win situation really.

2. Productivity

The main principle behind companion planting is the fact that when certain plants are grown together, then they benefit from one another, or at least the different plants can be grown together because they have different needs. This means that they are not competing for the same nutrients, or even atmospheric conditions.

With this being the case, then it also means that you can have a greater volume of plants in the same growing area, as they can be grown closer together without it being detrimental in any way – in fact if done correctly they will actually benefit from this closeness.

3. Easy maintenance:

The reason that companion planting generally means easier maintenance, may not at first be recognized. However the fact is that if the plants are chosen properly it means that they are planted closer together; meaning less of an area to cover when maintaining or harvesting your vegetables. This is especially relevant in a raised bed situation, where the area you have to cover is limited to the confines of the raised bed.

In this situation you have a 'double score' so to speak; as a raised bed garden is not so prone to weeds anyway, this coupled with correct companion planting, where the sunshine and nutrients are denied to weeds; leads to a situation where you are able maximise your efforts and get better results.

4. Natural insect control:
One of the big pluses for the companion planter is the fact that fewer insect problems occur, if the plants accompanying their neighbours are correctly chosen. For instance, if onions or leeks are planted alongside carrots, then problems with the dreaded carrot fly are less of an issue as the smell of the onions detracts the fly from the carrots.

Marigolds planted alongside your tomatoes will attract hover flies, which will protect them against aphids.
More examples to follow!

5. Less need for fertilizer
Again, if done correctly using organic methods of growing your vegetables, then there will be little if any need for fertilizer.

The reason is two-fold. Firstly good organic compost in your growing area means that fertilizer should not be needed unless you are perhaps aiming to grow 'super crops.'

Secondly; if the plants are rotated properly, then the needs of one plant may in fact be supplied by the waste or productivity of another. For instance legumes like peas and beans are able to draw nitrogen from the atmosphere and deposit it into the ground. This benefits a multitude of other plants who flourish in a nitrogen-rich soil.
More of this 'fertile partnership' in later chapters.

The influence of Allelopathy:

Firstly you may be forgiven for saying to yourself "What the heck is Allelopathy?" It is not after all the kind of word that comes up in every day conversation!

However there is a fairly simple explanation. Allelopathy is in fact a process by which an organism produces bio chemical's that are beneficial to other organisms, for their growth or development.

These bio chemicals are called allelochemicals and can be either beneficial (positive Allelopathy) or detrimental (negative Allelopathy) to the target organisms – i.e. your vegetables.
In fact even the detrimental effects of plants can play an important part in any natural defence program against herbivores for instance, as they discourage grazing animals from eating your crops.

Allelopathy is characteristic of certain plants, bacteria, algae, coral, and fungi; and Allelopathic interaction between the species plays an important part in the success of many plant species.

Resource competition also plays a part in Allelopathy, as the various plants compete for the elements (water, light, or nutrition) that is required for their survival. Although not strictly speaking negative Allelopathy, this plays a part when deciding which plants to choose as companions between the species.

Allelopathy is playing an important part in researching different environmentally friendly ways of controlling weeds, or making crops more productive; without so much dependence on chemical fertilizers or insecticides.

Again, this is nothing new, and in fact as early as 300B.C. Theophrastus noted the inhibitory effects of pigweed on alfalfa crops; while in 1st century China 267 plants were recognised as having pesticidal properties that could be beneficial to other plants.

Peas and beans add much needed nitrogen that will benefit many plant species

Why Plants Grow Well Together:

To be a little more accurate here we have to look at what we mean by 'grow well together' in other words, in what way are they beneficial to one-another's growth pattern. There are in fact three main ways that this can be so, and they are:

1. Nutritional

2. Protection

3. Decoy

Nutrition:
In the first instance, nutrition is perhaps the first thing that springs to mind when it comes to advantageous companion planting; and indeed nutrition is of paramount importance in most cases.

Beans and peas, as in all legumes, draw in nitrogen and fix it into the soil. This in turn can provide the nutrients for corn for instance; which in turn can act as stalks for the beans.

If squash is planted around the stems then this will benefit from the nitrogen, and in turn cover the ground with their broad leaves, restricting the growth of weeds and other competitors for the nutrients. This is the typical 'three sisters' approach to companion planting.

Another good example is the 'square foot' gardening approach. This is especially applicable to raised bed gardening, and is a simple rotational method of growing crops in a confined space (16 square feet), that are beneficial to each neighbour, and so produce good vegetables without the need for fertilizers.

Protection:
However there are the issues of protection against insect or herbivore predation to consider, and this goes hand in hand in many cases with the 'decoy' aspect of companion planting.

Even protection against inclement weather plays a part in companion planting. For instance some plants prefer the shade, and so can grow under the shade provided by tall plants like Tomatoes. This can also provide protection against high winds or other weather conditions, that may be detrimental to some fruit or vegetable species.

Insects:
Insects can be controlled either by using the natural insect repellent abilities of some plants to scare the insects away; or by using the natural attraction of some plants to insects

like aphids for instance; in order to encourage the aphids to attack this plant rather than the one you are promoting. Marigolds for instance attract the hoverfly, who's larvae eat aphids from carrots or tomatoes.

Nasturtiums are a classic example of this, and they are widely used to draw away aphids and other destructive pests. For this reason Nasturtiums are often referred to as sacrificial or Martyr plants, as they suffer in order to protect others.

These will be cover fuller in the examples below this article, where plants that grow well together, will be listed alongside the reasons why this is the case.

It is generally accepted amongst organic growers that planting masses of the same vegetable in long rows or concentrations is a bad idea. This is because by doing so you are attracting the predators of that one species from miles around – a bit like hanging a sign up and saying 'come and get me!'
Best practice is to intersperse your crops with herbs and/or flowers that protect your crop by disguising the smells and sights that attract the insects.

Plants That Grow Well Together:

Here is a list of plants that grow well together, with a brief explanation of just why this is the case. Although this list is not by any means an exhaustive list in itself; it only takes a little imagination to bring different species together, when you have the most basic gardening skills; and the knowledge that is contained in these notes to guide you.

Asparagus:
Best companions include: Tomato, parsley and Basil; and French marigold planted alongside will deter beetles. If on its own or just with Tomato plants, then Comfrey can be planted around as a good source of nitrogen for both plants.

Beans:

Companions include; Beetroot, cabbage, celery, carrot, cucumber, corn, squash, pea's, potatoes, radish, strawberry. Beans produce (draw from the air) nitrogen that is beneficial to the other plants
Nasturtium and rosemary can deter bean Beatles, while Marigolds can deter Mexican bean Beatles.

Cabbage Family:
Companions include; cucumber, lettuce, potato, onion, spinach, celery.
Chamomile and garlic can be grown to improve growth and flavour.
Marigolds and Nasturtium can be grown alongside to act as decoy for butterfly's and aphid pests. While mint, rosemary and sage will also deter cabbage moth and ants – as well as improve flavour.

Marigolds planted next to carrots attract hover flies, who's larvae in turn eat aphids. The smell of the marigold flowers also confuse the carrot fly

Carrots:

Good companions include beans, peas, onions, lettuce, tomato, and radish.

Including chives in the area will improve flavour and growth, while onions or leeks will distract the carrot fly by masking the scent of the carrots; as will sage or rosemary.

Celery:

Bean, tomato and cabbage family make good companions for celery.

Nasturtium, chives and garlic deters aphids and other bugs.

Corn:
Good companions are Potato, pumpkin, squash, tomato and cucumber.
French marigold deters beetles and attracts aphids from tomatoes.

Cucumber:
Good companions include, cabbage, beans, cucumber, radish, tomato.
Marigold and Nasturtium are good for attracting to themselves, aphids and beetles. Oregano is a good all round pest deterrent.

Lettuce:
Cabbage, carrot, beet, onion, and strawberry are all good companions for Lettuce.
Chives and garlic discourage aphids.

Melon:
Companions include pumpkin, radish, corn, and squash.
Marigold and Nasturtium deters bugs and beetles, as does oregano.

Onions:
Good Companions include the cabbage family, beet, tomato, pepper, strawberry, peas, and chard.

Chamomile and summer savoury helps improve growth and flavour. Pigweed brings up nutrients from the subsoil, and improves conditions for the onions.

Parsley:
Good companions include asparagus, tomato and corn.

Peas:
Good companions include beans, carrot, corn and radish. Chives and onions help deter aphids, as does nasturtium. Planting mint is known to improve the health and flavour of peas.

Peppers:
Tomato, eggplant, carrot and onion are known to be good companions for peppers.

Potatoes:
Good companions include, bean, cabbage, squash and peas. Marigold makes a good general deterrent for beetles, while horseradish planted around the potato patch gives a good overall insect protection.

Pumpkin:
Melon eggplant and corn make good companions for pumpkin.
Oregano and Marigold give a good all round insect protection.

Radish:
Companions are carrot, cucumber, bean, pea, melon. Nasturtium planted around is generally accepted to improve growth and flavour.

Squash:
Companions include melon, pumpkin, squash and tomato; while nasturtium and marigold; along with oregano, helps protect against bugs and beetles.

Strawberry:
Good companions include bean, lettuce, onion and spinach. Planting thyme around the border deters worms, while borage strengthens general resistance to disease.

Tomatoes:
Good companion plants for tomatoes include; celery, cucumber, asparagus, parsley, pepper and carrot.
Basil and dwarf marigold deter flies and aphids; mint can improve health and all round flavour.

These are some examples from popular vegetable types, and offer a guide as to what to consider for your companion garden.
Next chapter takes a brief look at what plants do not grow well together for any number of reasons.

My Notes/To Do List

Plants That Do Not Grow Well Together:

There are a few reasons why some plants should not be grown alongside others if you are considering the organic method of growing your vegetables.
I mention particularly organic, because the general idea behind companion planting is to avoid the use of chemical pesticides and fertilizers whenever possible.

Some plants should not be grown together simply because they both attract the same pests or other predators, others because they make the same demands on the soil, leading to them both producing a poor harvest. Some plants grown close together may produce a damp environment that leads to fungal or other infection.

Here are some plants to avoid if possible when considering a companion for your veggies.

Beans:
Should not be grown in the same vicinity of garlic, shallot or onions, as they tend to stunt the growth of the beans.

Beets:
Should not be grown along with pole beans, as they stunt each other's growth.

Cabbage
Is generally thought not to do well near tomatoes, mainly because the tomato plant can shade the cabbage. Avoid planting near radishes, as they do not grow well together.

Carrots:
Avoid planting near dill as this can stunt growth. Dill and carrots both belong in the Umbelliferae family, and if allowed to flower it will cross-pollinate with the carrots.

Corn:
Avoid planting corn and tomatoes together, as they both attract the same tomato fruit-worm.

Cucumber:
Sage should be avoided near cucumber, as it generally injurious to the cucumber plant.

Peas:
Onions and garlic stunt the growth of peas.

Potatoes:
Tomatoes and potatoes should not be planted together as they attract the same blight.

Radish:
Avoid planting hyssop near radishes.

Beneficial Herbs:

There are many herbs that can be extremely beneficial for your companion planting. Indeed the herbs themselves can lend that extra dimension to your vegetable garden, that will complement your vegetables – and improve your cooking!

Here is a list of some popular herbs along with the benefits they may have to certain plants.

Anise:
Anise is known to benefit beans and coriander plants.

Basil:
This is known to benefit asparagus, beans, cabbage and especially tomatoes.
It can be beneficial also as a 'sacrificial' plant in that it's soft leaves tend to attract butterflies and boring insects.

Caraway:
This is an ideal herb for breaking down and conditioning poor soils. It also attracts the attention of wasps and other harmful insects, making it a good 'sacrificial' herb. Also known to benefit strawberries and peas.

Chives:

An ideal companion for carrots, as it confuses the carrot fly. Also good around peppers, potato, rhubarb, squash or tomato plants, as it deters insects – particularly aphids.

Fennel:
This makes a **poor** companion plant for just about anything – avoid planting near other plants.

Lavender:
A good companion plant for many species as it's aromatic flowers attract many beneficial, pollinating insects to the garden.
It will also deter fleas, ticks and even mice!

Mint:
This is another all-round beneficial companion for many plant species; and in particular, peas, cabbage and tomatoes.
Mint is known also to deter insects, and even mice from your plants.

Parsley:
Asparagus is known to benefit particularly well, when grown alongside parsley; but carrots, cor, sweet peppers are also good companions.
Avoid planting near mint or lettuce.

Peppermint:

A good companion as it attracts beneficial insects and repels ants, aphids and cabbage fly.

Rosemary:
Beans, broccoli, cabbage, carrots and hot peppers all benefit from being planted alongside rosemary.
Planting carrots and pumpkins nearby is not advised as rosemary makes a poor companion for them.

Thyme:
Many plants such as cabbage, eggplant, potatoes and strawberries will benefit from planting thyme nearby; as it attracts many beneficial insects to the garden including honey bees.
It is also accredited with chasing off tomato hornworm, cabbage worms and flea beetles.

My Notes/ To Do List

Top 5 Benefits of Raised Bed Gardening:

You may well ask why an article on container gardening, is included in this piece on companion planting? The answer is simple – they both go pretty much hand-in-hand, and have many mutual benefits in the whole field of organic or sustainable gardening.

Not everyone unfortunately, has the space needed to build a raised bed, and if that is the case then maybe the next chapter on container gardening may be off more interest. However please do not discount raised beds on this account – for many of the techniques are in fact interchangeable, and beneficial for better production.

1: Diversification:
With the concept of companion gardening in mind, diversification is a particularly relevant plus, when it comes to the idea of a raised bed garden. A raised bed allows for a more accurate method of planning your planting regime; particularly if you are following the 'square foot' method of gardening.

Crop rotation is particularly easy and effective with a raised bed, as everything is within hands reach. For many people the concept of a smaller growing area compared to say, a traditional garden plot; is much easier to get a grasp off and so work effectively.

For beneficial planting a raised bed is particularly simple, especially when considering herbs as the beneficial plants. In fact the close proximity of plants in a raised bed situation, actually calls out for a knowledge of companion planting, if the gardener is to avoid planting species that are not beneficial at all to one another.

2: Ease of operation:
There is no doubt at all that a raised bed, once built and established, is far easier to operate than a traditional vegetable plot.
The soil is fresh, and therefore mainly free from weeds for the first season at any rate. When weeds do come through, they are easy to manage because the soil is lighter, and the height of the bed itself makes it easier to manage.

General maintenance of the vegetables, as well as harvesting is easier for the same reason as above. The bed itself (usually 12-18" high) makes it much less of a back-breaking task when it comes to general servicing of your plot.

For the disabled or otherwise infirm, a raised bed system can be a real blessing as it allows access even from a wheelchair – provided the area around it has been kept clear, and any space between beds is built in to allow for the width of a wheelchair.

As beds are usually only 3 feet wide, this allows a user to reach into the center from both sides.
Building a raised bed with an edge of around 6 inches, is a good idea as it gives an immediate platform on which to lay tools, or sit on, or even put you glass on wine on!
Oh, and I almost forgot to mention – no more back-breaking double digging!

3: Pest 'free'
Ok, while not exactly pest free, raised beds are without doubt easier to keep pests away from. Quite apart from the

companion planting methods described above; the simple fact is that a raised bed is easier to erect a simple frame for netting around, or indeed covering with clear polythene to form a mini-green house. This can be used to bring on plants that prefer warmer climates, and can also deter flying insects.

The fact that your vegetables are raised off the ground, also means that they are not so prone to crawling critters, determined to snack on your precious veg.

What about slugs? Simple, tack some copper tape around the outside edge of the frame, and the slugs will no cross over to wreak their usual devastation. This is because slug-slime has a chemical reaction with the copper that means slugs cannot cross over it.

Even burrowing critters such as rats, mice or gophers; can be stopped by simply putting wire mesh on the base of the raised bed before it is filled in, thus preventing them from burrowing upwards to munch on your veggies.

4: More productive
A raised bed is generally far more productive than a traditional vegetable plot, for a number of reasons. The first is that the soil in a raised bed has been specially chosen by yourself; and should be 80% good well-rotted organic material, to 20% actual good quality garden soil.

This means that you are not trying to plant in poor quality, clay-filled soil that is perhaps poorly drained and full of weeds that are competing for the limited nutrients available.

The fact that coupling companion planting techniques, along with the ability to plant much closer together; means that you will produce a much higher yield, than you would in a traditional garden layout.
More time spent harvesting and less time spent pulling out weeds, must be a great result for any gardener.

5: Longer growing season
Because a raised bed is by definition, raised out of the ground; it warms up quicker in the early spring and catches the last rays ant the end of the season. The result of this, depending on where you live, can easily add another month on to the growing season; as you can plant much earlier, and continue harvesting your crops until later in the season.

This results in your plants generally being more productive, and you extending your gardening season! This means also that your whole growing regime can become much more cost-effective as your overall growing time is extended.

Other things to consider:
One of the important things to consider when you are building your raised bed, is the growing medium itself. I

deliberately describe it as 'growing medium' because it is not garden soil. The mixture of 80/20 above is an indication that the infill must be a mix of compost and soil, and not soil alone.

The reason for this is two-fold. First of all, you will be far more productive with your efforts, if you include a properly balanced mix of organic material into your raised bed. Secondly, if you just fill in your raised bed with soil alone, then it will turn into a solid mass within your frame-work, and as a result will (understandably) become less productive and more labour intensive to maintain.

Top 5 Benefits of Container Gardening:

To begin with, please do not think that container gardening is the 'poor mans raised bed,' as some would have it. The fact is that even a raised bed, is a type of container garden if you think about it. All you're planting is in effect 'contained' within the boundaries of the raised bed framework after all.

However, without meaning to be facetious – lets quickly move on to the benefits of container gardening.

1: It's mobile!
Unlike a raised bed or a traditional garden; a garden built around the idea of containers has the advantage of mobility. This means that you can move around you containers to get best advantage of the sunlight, or indeed the shade. When pursuing the ideals of companion gardening; this is particularly effective as you can move around say pots of herbs, in order to protect various vegetable species from insect attack.

If you use smaller containers that can easily be shifted, you can move them around a patio or decking area, for purely aesthetic reasons; for instance flowering chives make a particularly beautiful backdrop, As does lavender or many other scented herbs.

2: Limitless containers
When it comes to the things you can use for your containers, the choices are virtually limitless; and restricted only to your imagination and the overall effect you wish to achieve. Everything from costly ornamental pots, to garden pails and even paint tins can be used for growing in containers – just be sure there is no residue of the previous occupant hanging around inside!

Using containers can be seen as a viable way to recycle old material and prevent it rotting in a landfill somewhere. Old wheelbarrows make good containers for growing vegetables, as do old tyres piled up, lined and filled with compost. Not moveable like the smaller pots – but very effective nevertheless (Great for growing potatoes in a stack!)

3: Insect repellent
In the same way as raised beds are more insect repellent because they sit off the ground; containers have a similar advantage over ground grown veg, in that they can be raised off the ground and so not so vulnerable to creeping insect attack.

You can also paint around the pot rim with copper paint; this will keep the slugs at bay. Strawberries grown in this way can be particularly effective as they are free from the predations of slugs; and they are limited as to their spreading abilities.

4: Space preserving
Especially for those who are not fortunate enough to have a raised bed or a traditional garden area; container gardening is really suited to the gardener who has a limited space to grow in.
Even with a small patio or balcony; indeed within the confines of the house itself, it is possible to grow a range of fruit and vegetables in pots for very little cost.

The main thing to consider is the size (and position) of the pot compared to the plant's needs. Whilst a tomato plant needs a two gallon pail at least to grow effectively; a pepper plant can be grown in a simple plant-pot and produce a good harvest of hot peppers.

5: Its good for you!
Ok, that's a very broad statement admittedly; however the fact is that growing vegetables, whether in raised beds or containers is beneficial in a number of ways for the grower. There is the environmental issues to take into consideration, inasmuch as you are reducing your needs for plastic-wrapped vegetables from the store – thereby saving the planet from your pollution.

The health issues are self-explanatory in that you are producing your own food, so should know exactly what goes into it – unlike the produce in the stores.

The fact that you are picking the food from your own premises, instead of from a store where it has been stocked after maybe thousands of miles in transportation; means that you are reducing your own 'carbon footprint' to zero.

There is another aspect of container garden that should not be overlooked, and that is the versatility of container gardening; and in particular how it can be used alongside raised bed or conventional gardening in order to get the best results from each discipline. By this I mean that you can take your companion planting knowledge and use it by planting say marigolds or mint in containers, and then placing them alongside the plants that will benefit from them.

For instance you could place pots with onions or shallots in amongst your carrot patch to save them from the carrot fly. Or perhaps place pots with French marigolds under your tomato plants to save them from voracious greenfly.

Finally it has to be recognised even by the most negative sceptic, that gardening in general has a beneficial outcome, in that it is good for the purposes of relaxation. What better place to get away from the hassles that constantly bombard the mind; than by tending your garden – container or otherwise.

****

Creating Organic Compost:

When it comes to making a good organic compost, there is the quick way and the longer way. If you are about to build your raised bed garden, or indeed fill in your pots already – then no doubt you will be looking for the quick way!

Quick organic compost:
First of all you need some well-rotted manure, preferably horse or chicken, then mix that with a good quality topsoil, mixed with general garden compost from the local garden center. I generally find that a mix of around 60% compost, 20% well-rotted manure and 20% soil makes for a good all-round growing medium.

This mixture may of course be changed, for instance if you wish to grow champion leeks, then heavier manure content should be considered.

Rotting leaves make ideal compost but do take some time to rot down properly.

Creating compost:

Compost takes time to mature, that is the hard facts of decomposition I'm afraid. However any serious gardener is always looking ahead at least one or two seasons, and preparing their growing plans accordingly.

To create your own compost; you should ideally have a composting bin, or a box arrangement that has a lid; this will keep away vermin, and prevent the rain from cooling down the compost.

A simple wooden structure made from recycled pallets will often make a very effective composting bin. Be sure that the opening is wide enough to allow for turning the contents with a garden fork occasionally to improve the composting process.

Material to consider for composting; can in theory be anything organic in nature, and includes such things as vegetable cuttings, tea bags, shredded paper, garden waste, grass cuttings, seaweed, comfrey leaves, kitchen waste, shrub cuttings, wood ash and fallen leaves.

If you have a good source of leaves available, then one of the simplest composters to make is perhaps the weld-mesh composter. Simply get some 2" weld-mesh cut from the roll so that it forms a tube about 18 - 24" across.

Cut so that there are wire ends that you can fold over, then bend the wire ends into itself where the end of the wire tube meets; so that it forms a permanent tube shape, then stand upright.

You should be left with a simple wire-mesh tube. This can then be filled with leaves to form a rich compost material.

If you make several of these tubes, they can even be arranged to form a kind of 'compost fence'- a great source of compost and a good talking point amongst the visitors!

Not everything organic is good for creating compost however, and material to leave out of the composter, include meat by-products, eggs or dairy products. Dog and cat dirt or litter, should never be put in the composter. Meat, bones or fish scraps should be kept out. Never put ashes from a coal fire into the composter, as this introduces sulphur to the mix.

<u>Small amounts</u> of wood ash is acceptable however as it introduces lime and potash, as well as magnesium and phosphoric acid, all of which are good for enriching the soil.

When adding or building up your compost, then it is a good idea to layer occasionally with some straw, garden soil, or fine twigs This all helps with the general aeration of the mix and the composting process.

Patience:
Something that can be in short supply for most people! It does however take patience to produce good compost, and usually a two year period will be required to get the best out of your composting efforts. The results however will show in the quality of your vegetables, and the general health of your garden.

Leaves and grass cuttings can take a particularly long time to fully rot down. How do you know if the material is well rotted? In general terms, well-rotted material should have a healthy earthy smell, and not smell like it is still rotting! It will be crumbly in your hand, and not be over wet and cloggy.

After all that effort, then you will also have the feel-good factor in knowing that you have done your bit for the environment – never to be underestimated!

Measuring volumes:
If you're buying bagged soil and making your own mix, here is an indication of what you may require. To use a 4' x 4' bed that is 12" high for the example; you first want to get your volume. Remember that 1 cubic yard equals 27 cubic feet. And to get your bed volume multiply the width, length and height in feet.

4 x4 x 1 = 16 cubic feet. This is how many cubic feet of soil your bed will require. If you're buying 2 cubic foot bags then the bed will take 8 bags, if you're buying 1 cubic foot bags, then it will take around 16 bags.

A raised bed measuring 6 foot by 3 foot and 18 inches high for instance, would take 27 cubic feet of compost. A simple calculation will provide the volume you need for whatever size of raised bed you may have.

My Notes / To Do List

Book 2:

Raised Bed Gardening Planting Guide – Growing Vegetables The Easy Way

Introduction to Raised Bed Gardening

"The love of gardening is a seed once sown that never dies." --
Gertrude Jekyll

You may well be wondering why on earth a raised bed garden is any easier than planting vegetables straight into the soil. Or why indeed I have titled this as I have done, by insinuating that raised bed gardening is easy.

Well the fact is that in my opinion, growing vegetables in a raised bed is by far the easiest way of growing great vegetables without the huge labour involved when growing the traditional way.
However I must clarify that by saying raised bed gardening has been around since the beginning of time, and although it has received more prominence as of late, it is by no means a new concept – think of the hanging gardens of Babylon !

Nothing however is without its cost, in both labour and financial expenditure, and it is true that to grow vegetables in a raised bed requires an element of both, especially at the early stages. This however need not put anyone off the idea, as the effort is minimal and short lived compared to the benefits derived from a raised bed garden that 'produces the goods'.

In this publication I intend to spell out, in layman's terms, just what it means to grow vegetables (or fruit, flowers etc) in a raised bed. How to construct a raised bed, simply and easily, including the different materials that can be used at minimal cost wherever possible. Even how to convert your raised bed into a temporary greenhouse, at minimum cost in easy to follow steps.

The raised bed gardener is able to spend longer tending to his plants than the average vegetable gardener, simply because he (or she) is not spending their valuable time digging over soil and clearing out weeds. For this reason alone the raised bed is preferable for those who are working all day and have limited time to spend in the evening tending their vegetable plot.

Advantages of a raised bed garden

There are several advantages that a raised bed has over planting straight into the ground, some of these are as follows:

With a raised bed, it really does not matter what quality your garden soil is, or indeed what the drainage is like. As this is all added when forming your raised bed garden.

Easy to service/maintain. With a raised bed you have the advantage of height, which means that you do not have to bend over as far to take care of your vegetables. This is particularly advantageous if you are prone to suffer from back-ache.

Weed free. A raised bed is not troubled to nearly the same extent by the incursion of weeds, as all the soil/compost mix is freshly added. For any weeds that do appear, they are easier to remove as the compost mix does not compact like garden soil.

It is far easier to control destructive pests within a raised bed garden. This is simply because you are off the ground, and so keeping a natural barrier up in front of creeping pests like garden slugs.

With a slightly higher raised bed of around two feet, then you are not troubled quite as much with carrot fly for instance, who tend to be low fliers.

So out with back-breaking weeding tasks, along with digging over water logged soil and filtering out rocks and stones. In with easy gardening methods for the busy householder, and fresh vegetables for the whole family with the minimal of hassle.

Building A Raised Bed Garden

"When the world wearies and society fails to satisfy, there is always the garden."-- Minnie Aumonier

A raised bed can be built with any one of a number of materials, the most popular being timber (untreated). Other materials include, concrete, brick, corrugated sheet metal or concrete block work. In fact anything that you have to hand that can produce a decent barrier about 1 foot to 18 inches high, can be used for a raised bed.

Raised Bed Dimensions:

As to dimensions, this is really determined by many things including the space you have available, and indeed just exactly what your requirements are. Do you have a large family to feed, or do you intend to sell or barter (bartering is a great way to enjoy a diversity of produce from other gardeners) some of your produce ?

With all that considered, a typical raised bed vegetable plot is about 6 foot by 3 foot. This is an ideal size because it allows access from both sides, without you having to step onto the raised bed itself. This enables you to tend to your plants without treading on them in the process – always a good thing !

As to depth, overall you should aim for 1 foot minimum depth, up to two feet for deep rooted plants such as carrots for instance.

The depth of the raised bed does not have to be the height of the sides, to explain a bit further. Say you would like a bed depth of 18 inches (450mm), but you only have timber for 12 inch sides. Simply build your bed in the manner described later, and dig out the interior an extra six inches. This will enable you to fill in the bed with the compost of choice up to the required depth.

It should perhaps be pointed out here though, that this negates the concept of building a raised bed for the advantages to be gained with the height of the bed itself above ground, as will be explained later in the article. This system is mainly used where the existing soil is of poor quality and has to be replaced/substituted in order to grow the vegetables of your choice.

If you are building multiple raised beds, then they should be placed about two feet (600mm) apart if possible, to allow for easy access between them.

Building a timber raised bed

The construction of a timber raised bed is fairly simple and straight forward. First of all, level and mark out the area where you would like your raised bed to be. Bear in mind that it should not be under overhanging trees, and in an area where you can have easy access for tending your plants. It should get a minimum of 5-6 hours sunshine per day to produce best results for most vegetables.

For a 6 x 3 x 1.5 foot bed built using traditional decking timber, you will need:

8 lengths decking @ 6' x 6" x 1"
8 lengths decking @ 2'10" x 6" x 1"
10 – 3" x 2" pointed posts @ 30"
Weed control fabric
Galvanized screws or nails
Wire mesh (optional)

Begin by marking out with string and pegs, the area of your raised bed, putting down a peg on each corner. This is where you should consider whether or not you are going to dig out any of the existing ground.

Questions to ask yourself are, what depth of compost do I need, versus what height do I want the finished bed to be. If you are growing root vegetables that need depth, but you do not want the finished height to be over 1 foot for instance, then digging out the area to the depth required is your only option.

Once this decision is made, then we can proceed with building the raised bed. Once you have the pegs in the area that marks out the four corners of your raised bed, you simply take out one peg at a time and replace by hammering down your pointed posts, leaving them a minimum of 18 inches above the ground.
Alternatively, if you make these posts longer then you can use them as handy aids for lifting yourself up when tending your vegetables – just a matter of choice really.

The best way to do this is to put down one post at the end, then temporarily fix the first short end against the post. With this done, then hammer in the second post flush with the end of the 6" x 2" decking plank. Proceed with the two longer sides, then complete the other end. If you just put one screw partially home, then you can easily adjust to suit.

Be sure that you have leveled the timber and that you have left a minimum 12" in height above the first planks, so you are able to complete the job.
I find that it is better to construct with a cordless screwdriver as this does not impact the framework in the same way that hammer and nails does. Also should you make a slight error, then it is no trouble to take apart for adjustment.

Once this is done then simply mark out along the inside length two feet from each end, then making sure the construction is straight, hammer in two of the posts to the same height as the others. On the end of the construction, do the same with one post in the centre of the framework.

This will give you a strong sturdy construction, which you will need if you do not want the sides of your raised deck to bow under the pressure of the soil.

Point of note:

If you are building with heavier timbers, say 6" x 2" for instance then it may be possible to just put one post in the center of the long side and none at all on the end. I however tend to lean on the cautious side, and would rather aim for stronger option overall. Another tip is to put a cross brace in, if you are concerned about the sides bowing outward.

It is not an exact science, but there are minimum guidelines that must be kept to ensure a construction fit for purpose.

After you have built the sides then just screw down the remaining planking face down along the edge (as in the photograph), to make a comfortable sitting or leaning area for tending to your raised bed.

One thing to consider during this time, is whether or not you are bothered by Gophers or Moles. If you are, then at this point you would place in 1" galvanized wire mesh, covering the bottom of your raised bed. This will be extremely effective in stopping the varmints from destroying your crop and giving you endless grief and heartache!

The weed control fabric should be fixed down the inside of the bed, to keep the wet soil away from the timber. This will help the timber to breathe and make it just that bit longer lasting.
Point of note: Do not use timber that has been treated with creosote, as this may weep through and kill the plants.

Building a raised bed from brick

If you are fully convinced that the position of your raised bed is permanent or that you will never need to move it to somewhere else; then the option of building a solid brick construction is open to you.
The advantages of a brick-built raised bed are simply that it will not rot, and is a sound structure not easily damaged. Disadvantages are that of course, you cannot move it to another position without destroying it, and also it can look quite unsightly depending on the surroundings. If for instance you have a brick-walled garden, then it may blend in very nicely.

Materials that you will need for your brick-built raised bed are as follows, based on a 6 x 3 construction:

Approximately 400 common brick
Sand and cement
Crushed gravel
Concrete ballast

With any brick construction then you have to build a foundation, otherwise the construction will crack as it subsides into the ground. This is quite a simple construction overall, but you may feel more comfortable getting a builder to do it if you have no experience at this sort of thing. However if you are at all interested, I would suggest that it is a good time to try out your building skills!

Begin by marking out and leveling the ground, as in the preceding chapter. When this is done, then dig out a trench for your foundation, bearing in mind that the brickwork has to be roughly centre of the foundation. The trench should be about 12 inches deep (for frost cover) and 12-18 inches wide, if you are building with 4" brick. This allows for a good concrete raft to build upon. If you are building in an area not bothered by penetrating frost then this trench can be shallower – or deeper if you have the opposite problem.

Mix up a concrete mix with your concrete ballast using a 5 – 1 mixture. That is 5 parts ballast to 1 part concrete. Add water and mix thoroughly. Fill the bottom of the trench a minimum of 3 inches deep with this concrete mix. This will ensure a good solid foundation for your construction.
In just a couple of days this will be dry enough to proceed with the building process.

Top Tip:
If you want to shortcut this process a little, then for this construction it is possible to simply lay 4" concrete block on a bed of cement mix, to form a ready-made foundation for your walls.

Once the foundation has been laid then it is time to put your building skills to the test. Main thing here if you have no experience with building is to string a line along the edge of your construction, and follow it. **Keep the spirit level at work** and be sure not to deviate from the line.

Mix up your sand and cement to a 3 to 1 mix. Three parts sand to one part cement. Add a plasticizer to the water before using as this will make things a lot easier when it comes to spreading the compo. Cement mix should be about ½ inch deep and the same at the ends. Each brick must be laid level, with a slight tap to bed-in. Be sure to overlap each brick as you are building, and tie in at the corners.

On the first layer to rise above the ground level, you should include a few 'weep holes'. This is simply done by keeping a couple of bricks without compo at the joints and leaving a gap instead.

Once you have reached the full height, you can either just finish off with a bed of cement over the top bricks, smoothing to form a half curve. Or you can finish with a concrete coping from the builders suppliers.

Dry stone raised bed

Actually made from concrete block, laid flat; this is a simple construction that can be taken down when and if, it's not needed any longer.

If you use 18" x 9" x 4" dense block, then layout a flat area for the base, pounding in some crushed rock for a foundation. After making sure your foundation track is perfectly level, using a straight edge; Start to lay your block on the flat side down on a bed of rough sand.

This row must be perfectly level otherwise you will face problems as the structure rises. Make sure that you overlap the blocks so that there is no break going up through the wall.

The down side with this raised bed is that you will use twice the concrete block as building normally, however you will save on sand and cement as well as time.

Drywall Example Above

Finished result should be a solid construction that has a good broad top to sit on while working your raised bed. True, it takes up a bit more space, but overall it is perhaps the simplest and quickest way to build. Just be sure of the first layer, and everything else will follow on.
Be sure that you tie in the corners using the same building method.

Top Tip: If you would like a more secure finish, then simply lay the top row of block on a bed of cement mortar. This will secure the whole structure quite nicely

Other raised bed examples

There is actually no limit to the amount of ways to construct a raised bed garden area, or indeed the different materials that can be used for it. Or perhaps I should say that the only real limit is your imagination!

Corrugated iron sheeting, properly supported is often used to create a raised bed. It has to be said though that if you are building for appearance, then this is probably not the one for you !
Timber logs cut straight from the tree. These can look especially effective and can be built similar to a log cabin construction, giving an extremely strong and versatile structure that will last for many years.
Old Railway sleepers. I would not particularly recommend using old railway sleepers, as there is a danger of creosote leaking into your plant bed, causing a health hazard – as well as killing the plants. If old sleepers are used then be sure to line the inside with polythene barrier to prevent this happening.

In general however the **modern railway sleepers** for sale in your local garden centre will not have been treated with creosote, but with a plant-friendly injection treatment. This makes them ideal for raised bed construction. Rot – resistant cedar or redwood are the best railway ties for building your raised bed. Consult the sales person before purchasing.

Build using the same principles above for the timber raised bed, but because of the heavy timber (about 19" x 5") you need only use support at the corners, except for the really long lengths at over 3 meters.

Filling and Modifications

Let my words, like vegetables, be tender and sweet, for tomorrow I may have to eat them. - **Author Unknown**

Filling the raised bed:
Next we come to filling your raised bed. This starts with the drainage at the base. This can be broken pots or rough broken brickwork, built to about three inches deep. However before this you may want to consider whether or not you are bothered by moles, gophers, voles etc.
These creatures are likely to follow the worms or fresh shoots up into your raised bed if you allow it to happen.

If you are in any doubt then lay out your 1" galvanized wire mesh at the base of the bed, before putting in your drainage level – better safe than sorry ! Also a layer of tough weed suppressant material at this stage, laid over the mesh will help keep out the burrowers

Once you have laid out your mesh, then put in the layer of drainage as described above. If you have a well-drained soil around you, or under the bed then this can naturally be adapted to suit.

The drainage should then be layered over with 3-4 inches of soil mixed with compost.
The compost itself, will largely depend on what you are about to grow. For instance, if you are growing carrots or parsnips, then a light loamy compost with a good mix of

sand may be required. Potatoes or leeks may require a good bed of well-rotted manure layered over the soil at the base.

It should be pointed out that the internal filling of any raised bed should not be soil alone, as this has a tendency to go rather solid after a short time. Instead mix some quality topsoil together with a good loamy compost, with plenty of organic material to keep it well drained. Again depending on your choice of vegetable a slow release fertilizer or well-rotted manure should be mixed through.

Hard work?
Ok, to be fair you may well be thinking that this sounds like a lot of hard graft – for something that is supposed to be an easy gardening method ? Well yes you could be right…However, once this part is done then you can relax and actually enjoy the next part, which is planting your vegetables. From now on it's easy street !

At this stage, and throughout the growing season you will discover just why raised bed gardening is so much easier than the traditional vegetable garden. Look over at your neighbour breaking his back hoeing between the vegetables, or digging his way through stony ground. Whilst all the time you are sitting on the side of your raised bed easily pulling out a few weeds, and plucking your ripe tomatoes.

Modification1 – Cold frame
One of the simplest and yet most rewarding conversions you can make to your raised bed garden, is to turn it into a

cold-frame. This will enable you to get an early start in the growing season with all your early plants such as tomatoes.

If you stay in colder northern climes, then this can become an almost permanent answer to a greenhouse, enabling you to grow things like cucumbers, marrows, chillies and tomato plants – to name just a few.

To do this is quite simple and will any take a short time. Start before you infill the raised bed with any compost material as it will be much simpler. Material needed for the job:

1 ½ " plastic pipe
Galvanized pipe straps
½" flexible pvc tubing or similar
Polythene sheeting

Cut out eight lengths of 1 ½" plastic pipe, the kind used for domestic plumbing is just fine, measure so that they do not protrude above the wall of the bed when placed vertically inside.
Next space evenly along the inside wall of the bed, pointing upward, and secure in place using galvanized pipe straps, top and bottom.
When this is done then cut the ½ " tubing to about twice the width of the raised bed. Bend the pipe and slip into place.

To stop the bent tubing slipping all the way down the pipe, simply fill with some fine gravel or even a sand and cement mix up to about 4" (100mm) from the top of the pipe. Once this is done you will have an effect similar to the covered wagons you see in the old western movies !

Next you simply fit the polythene over the framework. This is easiest done by securing the polythene sheet along one side of the frame by a length of 2 x 1 for instance. Then you simply pull over the frame when you want it covered. The ends are a bit more awkward, but if you leave plenty material to work with, then you can simply weigh down by placing a plank on top of the polythene, and weigh down with bricks or equivalent.

The following picture below shows a smaller version of that described, but using just a part of the raised bed area.

One thing you may note is that this model can be improved by the addition of slits or vent holes in the polythene. Better still fit it with polythene that has holes in it especially for the purpose, as in the example above where only part of the raised bed is used for bringing on the seedlings.

This style of perforated polythene will prevent your 'polytunnel' from overheating.
Failing that then you must remember to remove or fold back the sheeting when appropriate. This is especially true if your intention is just to use it for the hardening of young plants.

Modification 2 – Insect/Bird netting
Another good thing about the raised bed is just how easy it can be covered up to stop the predations of birds or insects. The simplest way to do this is to follow the previous example for creating the frame effect, but replacing the polythene with a fine bird mesh.

This can be easily clipped into place in a few minutes, keeping your plants free from not only birds such as wood pigeons, blackbirds etc; but also stopping the cabbage butterfly for instance, from laying it's eggs on your plant leaves.

Another way however to do this is to follow the example in the picture.

This is an old kids swing frame, that handily fits right over the raised bed.

This in turn gives you a structure that you are able to walk around in, whilst tending your vegetables.

It would only take a simple modification to convert this into a temporary greenhouse, if you used polythene instead of nylon mesh.

Yet another way to cover up, is to raise up a post on each corner of the raised bed, link together with a 2 x 2 along the top, between the four corners.
This will give you an effect like a four poster bed, which you can then cover with your material of choice.

As you can see, there are several ways to cover your raised bed, either to use as a cold-frame or to simply protect against birds and insects. All these ways will only take a very short time, and will reap great rewards.

Modification 3 – Automatic Irrigation

Another addition to your raised bed can be an irrigation system. This can be an automatic irrigation system, or it can simply be a system that is put in place, and watered when you choose to do so. There are many watering systems on the market, but here is a simple model to follow that will do the job fine.

Place ½" polythene pipe under the soil just an inch or so, shaped like a tuning fork, with the single end at the top attached to a fitting such as a 'hoselock' click fit type. This can simply and easily be put together with 2 push fit elbows and 1 tee piece. 2 end caps close of the end of the pipes
The pipe should be perforated along it's length with small drip emitters fitted every 12 inches.

After fitting a stop valve at the raised bed end, the whole system should them be fitted to a water tank - the bottom of the tank raised above the top level of the bed.

This tank can be attached to the mains water supply if needed, or it can be filled manually. with a float valve to close it of when the supply is not needed.

By turning the water valves on, the drip emitters will release a small amount of water over any given period. After some 'fine tuning' this is a system that will take away a lot of the labour attached to watering a vegetable garden.

Working Tips For A Raised Bed

When is a cucumber like a strawberry?
When one is in a pickle and the other is in a jam.

When it comes to tending a raised bed garden, there are a few differences, or subtleties compared to tending a traditional vegetable patch.

Here are a few tips for making life even easier !

Cut a strong 'spanner board' ie, a board that is slightly longer than the width of your bed. Place across the bed, resting on each side edge. This can be used for placing your small garden tools on when working the bed, without leaving them in the wet soil. A good place also to put a glass of something cool !

Avoid standing in the raised bed. This is to prevent the soil becoming compacted, and also to prevent any chance that you will push out the sides of the raised bed, by compressing the soil over time.

If you have multiple raised beds, then put down a weed restricting fabric between them and cover with 2-3 inches of mulching material such as chipped bark. This saves a lot of laborious weeding between the beds, and leaves more time for what really matters in life.

Plants can be grown a little closer together in a raised bed, because of the concentrated nature of the feeding system.

Another good tip and one that will keep the slugs and snails at bay, is to place a copper slug tape or strip around the timber structure. Slugs hate copper because of the way it reacts to the slug mucus, so they will not cross it. If you have no copper tape and have an immediate slug problem, try spraying a concentrated salt solution around the outside base of the bed. This can be quite effective, but do not let any into your plant bed as it will most likely kill your vegetables !

Working a raised bed garden as can be seen here is slightly different for the 'normal' way of gardening – but not so different that you need a new set of rule books so to speak. When speaking to raised bed gardeners, you will probably find that the biggest difference is the fact that they are not suffering from constant backache!

The raised bed is much easier when it comes to weed control – mainly because you have started by using virgin soil that is weed free to begin with. However even after it has been up a while, it is still much easier to weed owing to the softer loamier make-up of the soil or compost.

Even the feeding of the plants is more successful, as all the nutrients are going to the plants and not seeping away into the soil, as is normally the case.

Building multiple raised beds, if you have the space, is ideal. This allows for a good rotation of the different crops and guarantees a great harvest year after year.

Vegetables For A Raised Bed

This cabbage, these carrots, these potatoes, these onions ... will soon become me. Such a tasty fact!
   *- **Mike Garofalo***

What vegetables would I recommend to grow in a raised bed ? Just about anything !

Seriously, there is nothing I can think of that will not grow as well if not better in a raised bed, than it would in a traditional vegetable plot. The mere fact that the vegetables are raised up away from the creeping things of the soil, means that they have better protection against insects, and are not so prone to fungal disease as they have better air circulation in general.

For instance, cucumbers will grow better as they can be trailed over the edge of the bed, keeping them of the ground. Carrots are a crop where it is better to keep them raised anyway, in order to help protect from the carrot fly. Potatoes can be easier to dig up from a raised bed, as can parsnips and any deep rooted vegetables, simply because the soil is looser.

It is much easier on the back when tending strawberries or any low growing fruit or vegetable. However, tomatoes grow exceedingly well in raised bed situations, as they can greatly benefit from a concentrated feeding regime of the type a raised vegetable garden offers.

It is a simple matter to build any kind of trellis work on a raised bed – particularly the timber models, as it is easier to secure any fixings into. Growing beans or peas in a raised bed complete with trellis or framework is a simple matter when working a raised bed vegetable garden.

Summary
As you may have guessed by now, I am quite a fan of raised bed gardening. Yes it is true that more preparation is involved at the beginning of the project, if you are going to build a raised bed.
However the rewards in my view, are well worth the effort, as the raised beds that you build should give you many years' worth of service.

Another advantage of the raised bed that I have not covered here, is simply the fact that you do not need the same range of expensive garden machinery. Rotavators for instance, usually needed to dig over the soil, are not needed for a raised bed. Most of the digging work is done with the help of a small garden fork, as the soil is generally light and loamy.

In fact almost all the tools you need are simple hand tools, for light digging and pruning of your plants.

I have been asked in the past, just what is the difference between a raised bed and a planter – the answer is simple. A raised bed does not have a timber base, and therefore cannot be moved around. Planters do have a slatted base and are generally smaller, to enable positioning. Planters are generally chosen for ornamental purposes.

There are areas however where there is just a fine line between one and the other – and that is fine.

Final note of caution: Do not build a raised bed on a decking area – it's far too heavy, and will rot your deck. Choose a smaller planter instead.

My Notes / To-Do List

Book 3:

Vegetable Container Gardening Growing Vegetables In Containers & Planters

Chapter 1: Planting – Where Am I Coming From ?

"no-one is born in a vacuum and we are all molded by the circumstances in which we find ourselves" **anon**

I was born and brought up in the kind of family where money was always on the scarce side, and I was no stranger to making ends meet with whatever came to hand. Consequently although I may be accused of being on the mean side with the old cash flow, I would say in my defense that I was really just very careful with the somewhat limited funds at my command.

The benefit of being raised under these somewhat restricted circumstances, is simply that you are soaked deep down with the understanding that money is very hard to acquire, and painfully simple to throw away.

What does that have to do with vegetable container gardening you might ask ? Simple really; planting vegetables in containers can be a great way to get maximum value out of a limited space or resource, and if it is utilized properly you can even make junk turn you out a handsome profit.

Some people are put of the idea of growing their own vegetables because they do not have a garden, or a plot of land big enough to raise vegetables on. This is however a misapprehension, as the fact is that by following the right guidance you can provide a good supply of vegetables from a very limited space by utilizing the ideas in this manual.

As a child of about 11 years old, my father decided to move us lock, stock, and barrel to what amounted to a smallholding just a mile or so up the road from where we stayed in a rented council house. For us as kids it was a mixed blessing because on the upside we now stayed in a large house, with loads of garden space and some old out-buildings to play in.

However the downside was that from the get-go my father decided that we would learn his ways, from his childhood. This was not good news to us, as with this move he decided that we should 'pull our weight' and get to work on the farm.

Now you might think that with plenty of land available to plant in, we would have no need of growing vegetables in containers. However this was not the case as the fact is with a family of nine children to feed, every space has to be utilized to its best advantage, and every money-saving technique put into place. My parents were not wealthy, and so with good Scottish prudence put us to work around the smallholding.

Amongst the things I hope you will find interesting in this book, apart from tips on planting in containers; are things like how to renovate an old greenhouse on a tiny budget, how to grow vegetables in planters and raised garden beds as well as produce tomatoes, cucumbers and even grapes from an old grapevine!

Life "down on the farm" was not a barrel of laughs, it has to be said. There were times when my brothers and I would have done anything to get out playing football with our friends, or get away causing some mischief somewhere.

Instead however we were stuck on the farm, hoeing weeds out of the vegetable plots or mucking out pigs and horses. Not to mention chickens, geese, ducks, rabbits and all the other things associated with running a smallholding.

Not long after we moved into this smallholding, which was basically an old farm house with a couple of acres of land attached, my father decided that he was going to use a part of this ground to break up cars, as he was actually a car dealer by this point.

You probably think that I am wandering away from the point right about now! However it is all relevant, as will become clear later on in the book.

We soon discovered that even scrap cars can have their uses around the vegetable garden – strange but true. They have their dangers also when young children are around, as we soon discovered to our cost – however that is another story!

General repairs around the place had to be done of course, and this was when it was really discovered that I was particularly good with my hands (The brain was on vacation most of the time, so it was as well I was good at something!) Needless to say that rather than pay for experienced men to handle the tasks around the place, I was put into the "front line of defense" when a shed needed repaired or built.

As you can imagine on an old farm, there is always something needed repaired, so I was kept busy most of the time, much to my annoyance.

Yes of course mistakes were made – I was only 11 years old don't forget – but throughout this "school of hard knocks" experience, I learned a lot.

How to grow vegetables in containers – I first of all had to learn how to build planting containers, on a very limited budget, as you may well imagine.

Chapter 2: Time Rolls On

"Time is the coin of your life. It is the only coin you have, and only you can determine how it will be spent. Be careful lest you let other people spend it for you." Carl Sandburg

Yes, the years have moved on at an alarming rate, and now at 54 years of age I find myself writing this ebook, attempting to put some 43 years of knowledge into a few thousand words!

Most of it is thankfully irrelevant to this book, so at least you may be spared the ramblings and moaning's that are the lot of most people (so I am told) of my age.

Getting back to the point of this exercise; growing vegetables in containers or planters, is not rocket science. No matter what some of the manuals tell you, growing or planting anything, let alone vegetables, just needs the will to do it and the right conditions to it in, the results will come naturally.

Granted, if you are intent on growing prize tomatoes, or huge award-winning marrows, then a certain expertise is involved.
Being best at anything does not usually happen by chance, but rather by real commitment and dedication to the task – no matter what it is.

During most my so-called childhood, along with the rest of my brothers, I was busy between school and the farm. The summer was a curse of sorts to us, because while our friends were 'out and about' we had to work in the lighter evenings. At least during the darker winter evenings we could be out with our friends.

However, years later it turned out that I had in fact learned a few things about self-sufficiency. How to make the most of very little, and how to survive through tough economic times – like now.

Learning how to grow vegetables, was just a part of my upbringing. However it was a part that has an increasingly significant place in the world in which I find myself today; and one which I hope to share in this book.

Scrap Cars & Recycling:

I mentioned earlier, that even scrap cars have a role to play in the world of container gardening. Well the fact is that one of the most difficult parts of a car to re-cycle, are the tires. The steel wheels were always easy enough, as they are indeed scrap and so they were worth collecting and taking to the scrap merchants.

The tires though were another problem. Now however that problem can turn into an advantage, at least in a small part, because the tires can very easily be made into very good and productive planters, at zero cost to you.

Simply go down to your local car-breakers and most of the time they will gladly give you as many tires as you need, as they have to pay to get the tires taken away and disposed of.

When choosing your car tires however, be sure that they are all the same size, obvious I know – but it's very easy to forget the obvious sometimes and be left with a problem you don't want.

The different kinds of containers that can be used for container planting, as well as the construction methods employed where needed; will be discussed in the next chapter, as will the soil or compost mix and numerous details that must be taken into account to get the most out of your container garden.

Chapter 3:Planter Types and Ideas

"Necessity, who is the mother of invention." **Plato**

Often times the best ideas simply come when you have to think "outside the box" usually because you just cannot afford to pay shop prices for what you want. Such is the case for our first planter, discussed in the previous chapter – the tire planter.
This must be one of the simplest planters to construct as you are really just stacking tires one on top of the other.

As mentioned the tires should all be the same size, unless you want to have a tire that looks like it has a pot belly ! Normally there is no need to link them, as the weight of the soil itself will usually keep it all together.

However if you want to play it safe, all you need do is lay the tires one on top of the other until you have achieved your desired height. Then link them by boring through them with a drill or sharp awl, in three places. Tie them together with galvanized tie-wire or nylon string – job done.

The height of the planter depends on whether or not you need deep compost, this really depends on what you intend to grow.

A word of caution. Make sure that there is no contamination of the tires when you collect them from the breakers yard. Diesel in particular will kill your plants stone dead, ruin your entire day really!

Tire planter for Potatoes:

Tire planters make particularly good potato barrels. If you have not heard of this concept in potato growing, then it is simply this. Growing potatoes in a small area, is quite impossible using traditional methods, and this is where the potato barrel comes in.

By using your tires, start by placing three tires in the area where you plan to grow the potatoes, one on top of the other. (it cannot be moved later). **Do not link** these tires together, you will see later why. Make sure you have some drainage at the base (broken clay post or gravel will do fine) then fill up to the height of the second tire, with a good compost material.

Place your seed potatoes in place with shoots facing upwards (usually two or three seed potatoes will suffice) and cover over with a further 2-3 inches of soil or compost.

Place another tire on top, and wait for the shoots to break the surface by a further two or three inches. Put in more compost up to the top level of the shoots, with just a little breaking the surface.

Repeat this procedure, till the tires are about three feet tall, or starting to get unstable. When your crop is ready to harvest, you can simply pull apart your planter, easily revealing the mature potatoes ready for harvest.

Now you see why we did not tie the tires together, it would be a bit of a nightmare to harvest the potatoes if we did, as the nature of the tires means the compost gets a good grip inside, being filled with potatoes. This can make it incredibly difficult to get them out of the planter.

Other planter types that suit the potato barrel model are, the box wood planter that can have the sides removed to reveal the crop when ready. Then there is the simple plastic bag method. This gets cut up the side to easily remove the potato harvest. Then there is the barrel method where to harvest the crop you have to tip over the barrel completely to get the potatoes out.

All of these planters follow the same idea as to raising the soil level as the potato grows. All very successful, and extremely satisfying when it comes to harvest time.

Traditional Timber Planters:

Timber vegetable planters are very easy to construct, and indeed can be reasonably inexpensive. One of the cheapest ways is to go to the local sawmill if you have one, and as if they have any 'barks' available. These are the offcuts that are trimmed of the tree before it is cut into regular shaped planks.

I have built many things in the past for virtually nothing by using barks instead of expensive cut planks. Not just planters, but garden sheds can be built using this method.

Building with barks can look great, and really fit in with the surroundings a lot more naturally than finished timber can.

To be fair, there is some extra work sometimes, just squaring them of a bit. Depending on the load there can be a fair bit of waste also. However for the barks that are no use for construction, simply cut them to size for use in the log burner !

Building with treated timber however does have it's advantages in that it lasts longer and is quicker to construct, just because the timber is all of a uniform size.

Timber planters come in all sizes, but the construction methods are basically the same. It is not rocket science, and is in effect four or six posts, with planks nailed up the sides to the desired height.

A basic timber planter for instance may be six feet long (1,500mm) by 18 inches (450mm) wide by one foot (250mm) high. It is advisable to re-enforce with an upright post ever three feet, and so this planter for instance would have 6 posts, one in each corner and one in the middle on each side.

The base of the planter is best made from plant friendly treated timber (not creosote, which will kill the plants.), about 1 inch (25mm) thick at least. This will ensure a good few years from the planter.

The base should be raised a couple of inches from the ground, and have a few holes bored for drainage also, other-wise your plants will become waterlogged, which is no good unless you are growing rice!

Top tip – do not use plywood or chipboard for your planter as it will just burst. Stick to sawn solid timber if you want it to last.

A vegetable planter of this kind is really another adaptation of a raised bed, with the only real difference being that a planter can be moved around (though it will be extraordinary heavy when full), and has a raised base built in. A raised bed garden is fixed in place as the posts are sunk into the ground, and the raised bed is generally a wider construction.

Using an Old Wheelbarrow ?

Old wheelbarrows make excellent planters, especially if they still have a working wheel on them, as this enables you to follow the sun (or the shade), and makes for a truly mobile planter. A great advantage, if for instance the sun is only a short time in one area of your garden.

Be sure you punch a few holes in the base for drainage, as they easily get waterlogged. Painted up, a wheelbarrow can look good as well as "produce the goods" when it comes to growing vegetables or plants.

Another idea for a wheelbarrow, particularly if the base is rotten, is to prop it up on end against a wall, handles in the soil. With this you can now grow a climbing vine up the wheelbarrow, using it as a makeshift trellis. This can be really effective once the plant has taken hold.

If you do not have an old wheel barrow, then why not make a wooden one ? This can be particularly effective, and a real addition particularly to an ornamental garden, where the ascetics are important.

Traditional ornamental pots:

If you want to grow vegetables on your patio are for instance, it is probable that you would like something a bit more "pleasing to the eye" than a re-cycled ten gallon paint tin, or maybe an old kiddies bath (both can make very effective planter).

This is the time where you might spend some cash and buy an ornamental plant pot for a patio. Be sure that it is glazed if it is liable to be left outside in the frost, otherwise it will burst the first winter unless you overwinter it inside.

One of the advantages of an unglazed ornamental pot is that you can age a new pot quite effectively by brushing it over with yogurt or just milk. This will encourage the growth of algae to give it an old look.

Pots can look particularly effective if you are growing climbers like peas or beans for instance. Simply make a pyramid shape out of three canes, sunk into the compost and tied at the top. This will produce a good harvest and look very effective on your patio.

A word of caution. Clay pots can dry out very quickly, so be aware of this and water accordingly.

Black plastic pail planters:

Ok, so a black plastic pail does not make for a very attractive planter, granted. However the black plastic has an added advantage that it absorbs the heat from the sun, which in turn transfers to the compost.

This makes for good growing conditions for the likes of marrows, cucumbers, chilies and a host of other vegetables that prefer a bit of warmth in the soil.

Again, be aware of the fact they tend to dry out quite quickly and so need fairly constant watering.

Hanging basket planters:

Most people think of hanging baskets only for flowers, however they can be very effective also for vegetables or fruit such as strawberries. The fact they are hanging up in the air means that the dreaded slugs won't get to munch away at your strawberries – a fruit which they seem particularly fond of!

Wire frame hanging baskets are very cheap to buy, and can last many years if taken inside over winter.
One tip for hanging baskets is to make the chains a little longer than usual (you can buy chain at most handyman stores), and plant beans or peas to climb up the chains. This is a great system that will produce a good harvest very cheaply.

Planting in the gutter!

Ok, this is perhaps more for raising seedlings than growing a mature crop. Nevertheless old guttering is great for raising young plants, because you can take them out of the guttering with a simple cut with your trowel.

This means less disturbance for your young plants, which in turn means that they will transplant a lot more effectively, leading to a more successful crop.

There are a few things that you could grow to maturity in old guttering – lettuce for instance, or maybe a miniature herb garden ?

Guttering does tend to get waterlogged quickly when used outside, so best to run along the base and drill a few holes for drainage

Timber window boxes:

These are constructed in very much the same way as the timber planters mentioned earlier, but are usually built to fit the particular windows. Be aware when building, that window sills tend to be sloped away from the house.

This means that when you attach the wooden runners on the base to keep it clear of the sill, you put a corresponding slope on the runners so that the planter will sit level.

It may seem a small point, but it is simple to implement during construction, and means that you are not having to prop up the box with bits of slate to keep it level.

Since window boxes are meant to decorate the house, in most cases. A good option for planting here is the strawberry plant as they will not block out the sun from the interior of the house, and do produce a nice flower as well as great fruit of course.

Oh, did I mention – remember to water regularly as in all the examples before !

My Notes / To-Do List

Chapter 4: Container Planting Top Tips

Gardening requires lots of water - most of it in the form of perspiration. ~**Lou Erickson**

Compost for containers:

It is important when planting in a container that the conditions are just right, if you want to maximize your results. Containers in particular, because of their very nature are more prone to leaving a plant root bound, if they have been planted to close together. Just in the same way that a pot-plant can get root-bound.

The difference is that unlike the pot-plant, you cannot just re-plant your marrow or tomato plant should it get all root-bound.

Other things to watch out for when planting in containers is watering, mentioned several times in this article already. It is nevertheless one of the easiest things to get wrong, and so suffer a poor harvest or worse – a dead one!

How to avoid over-watering as well as under-watering will be looked at in this chapter.

The compost in planters, is just slightly different as that when growing straight into your garden bed for instance.

One of the main points to consider is not to use soil from the garden in a planter, as it tends to set hard in the planter.

Instead use a good mixture of compost and other material to keep the soil loose and aerated, more on this later.

What a plant needs:

First and fore-most a plant needs light to thrive, yes its true that some need more than others, but fundamentally vegetables in particular need plenty of light.

The leaves of the plant soak up the light, and are in fact the 'engine room' so to speak of the whole plant. The roots soak up the water, but the light is the real energy source that feeds the engine.

That said, this is one of the biggest advantages of container gardening. Simply that you can place your containers where the plant is getting the best light conditions available.

Bear in mind that "full sun" is considered to be around 6 or more hours per day. So all your calculations should be based around that figure.

Water conditions we have already explored, so no need to go into that further at this point. Just bear in mind that a plant will need different levels of water according to its needs, and the particular stage of growth. IE a tomato plant that if full of fruit will need more water than one that has yet to produce any. It's not rocket science!

Feeding your plants:

When it comes to feeding your vegetable planters, then the debate goes on as to whether or not to go organic, and dump the chemical fertilizers altogether.

Personally on this issue, I use organic fertilizer whenever I can, but understand that not everyone has access or the time to feed their vegetables with organic fertilizer on a regular basis.
Feeding organically, with the use of well-rotted manure for instance, takes a bit more preparation than just throwing a handful of 'growmore' at your vegetables. However I believe the results are worth the effort.

Well prepared compost should include where possible, a mix of well-rotted manure or composted material from your kitchen for instance. Mix this through with your 'store bought' compost if you have none of your own. This will ensure that your vegetables get a good start.

If you are using your own compost from your composting bin, be sure to take the compost from the bottom of the pile. This is 'the good stuff' and should be crumbly and definitely not wet or smelly. This would indicate the compost was not ready for planting.

Basically what you are doing is adding a balanced diet of .N(Nitrogen), .P(Potassium) and .K (Phosphorus) – the key ingredients to a happy plant!

If you are using a chemical fertilizer then you should look out for this designation on the box, where N.P.K is usually marked according to the mix.

Nitrogen loving vegetables like cabbage or spinach for instance like a higher percentage of .N in the mix, whereas peas and beans get their nitrogen from the air and so do not need a strong nitrogen based formula.

Most marketers of chemical fertilizers nowadays have this marked on the box, even designating the vegetable types that the fertilizer is best for.

Filling your planters:

As mentioned earlier, the material used to fill the planters cannot include your garden soil, unless it is of exceptional quality and of a loamy nature. The reason being is that soil in a planter tends to go firm, and makes it difficult for the plant to thrive.

To begin with make sure that whatever planter you decide on, has holes in the base for drainage. Planters do tend to get waterlogged very easily if there is no drainage built in, leading to stem rot or worse.

To complete the drainage part you have to scatter some gravel or crushed stone about one or two inches deep along the bottom of the planter, old broken clay pots are ideal for this. This will simply prevent the drainage holes from getting clogged up and made ineffective as a result.

Next is of course to add your compost mix, hopefully you have made up your own quality compost with a good mixture of compost and well-rotted manure. This will add the needed nutrients and also help keep the compost 'loose' enabling maximum root growth.

If you are planting in a hanging basket then of course the gravel or broken pot idea is redundant, simply line the basket cage with coconut fiber liner or whatever equivalent is available. Next it is advisable to line with a black plastic liner to prevent the moisture escaping entirely. Poke two or three holes to allow some drainage.
Fill in the basket with your chosen growing compost, perhaps with the addition of moisture retaining gel from the local supplier.

If you are using the organic method of manure versus growmore for instance, then mix your manure depending on the level that your vegetables require. Potatoes for instance like a good mix of manure, but peas on the other hand do not.

Depending on just what vegetables you plan to grow will by and large determine the kind of 'growing compost' mixture you should use to fill your planter. For instance root vegetables like carrots prefer a more sandy free-draining mixture.

Feeding:

Once you have your vegetables planted, then you must of course put in place a feeding regime if you are to get the best out of them. Because of the limited nature of the space involved in most planter's, feeding is highly recommended.

Mostly this is done with a liquid fertilizer during the stages of growth, perhaps with a light feed once per week or so, depending on the liquid feed used – refer to the manufacturer's instructions here if in doubt.

A slow feed granular mix can also be used, simply scatter lightly around the plant base and the watering in will do the rest. The main thing with the chemical feeds is not to over-do it, as this will do more harm than good.

Manure caution

Just a word of caution, is perhaps needed here. Never use dog, pig or cat manure on the garden or in your compost heaps or bins.

Certain parasites like worm larvae tend to stay for a while in this type of manure, and so it should never be used for growing vegetables.
Also it is a wise move if you are bringing in manure to know what the source is, is it a pig farm for instance?

For the record, sheep, cattle and horses make the best manure overall.

It goes without saying, that you should also keep pets out of the garden, especially cats – but you knew this already, right!

Finally, if you are spreading manure on the surface of the garden, then be sure that it is well rotted, and never spread around fruit like strawberries or vegetables like marrows and cucumbers as they will be laying amongst it, increasing any chance of contamination.

Mulching:

I am a keen advocate of mulching in general, it keeps out the weeds and keeps the soil around the plants moist even in the hot sun. Bark chippings are my favorite mulching material, for my flowers and vegetables.

For cucumbers, marrows etc I use just straw to mulch. This gives the vegetable a dry bed and discourages the dreaded slug.

However it has to be said that unlike planting in a garden or perhaps a raised bed; growing vegetables in planters usually means that there is not much space for mulching. However it is still worth-while, and perhaps more relevant when your planters are prone to dry out quickly.

Watering your planters:

OK, I guess everyone knows that plants need watering or they will simply die. But what exactly does water do to a plant? Three main things actually, they are:

Turgor, or rigidity. Water pressure within the stem of the plants creates Turgor so that a plant is able to stand.

Water enables the nutrients in the soil to energize the plant through the roots.

The process of photosynthesis means the plant uses light, carbon dioxide and water to make sugar.

As mentioned, planters are indeed prone to either drying out to quickly, or getting waterlogged by over-watering. Whether by nature or nurture-so to speak. Water logging blocks the oxygen source to the roots of the plant, and so the plant dies unless remedial action is taken in time.

Fungal diseases also thrive in wet conditions, making this a "double whammy" for the poor plant.

How do you know if your plants are over-watered? Well the tell-tale signs that a plant is getting too much water are:

Leaves yellowing from the bottom up

Soil turning green

Grey mold appears on the plant

Plant has stopped growing

Plant is wilting badly

Prevention of this is simple. Make sure that you have prepared your planter properly as per the earlier instructions. Do not be to enthusiastic when it comes to watering, but even if you are, proper drainage should allow for the soil to reach a natural level.

Be observant! just watch your plants for the signs of overwatering, and be ready to remedy the situation. If there is indeed fungal growth, then you may have to apply a fungicide to remedy it.

Under-watering signs include:

Dry, hard soil or compost

Plant leaves tend to go brown and crisp

Plant shrivels and dies!

You will notice the list here is shorter ? Fact is that many more plants die from overwatering than the opposite, largely because the overwatering starves the roots of oxygen and so the plant reacts faster in many cases.

My Notes / To-Do List

Chapter 5: Matching Planter to Plant

"It's difficult to think anything but pleasant thoughts while eating a homegrown tomato."~ **Lewis Grizzard**

Now that you have your planters all sorted out, you should be ready to get them planted out with the vegetables or fruit, flowers even of your choice.

This is quite a simple process, but requires some careful thought. For instance you must decide not only what you would **like** to grow in your planter, but also what can be grown with a reasonable expectation of success.

For instance if you live in Scotland, you should not expect to grow peppers or sweet corn in a planter, unless it was inside a greenhouse or cold frame.

Also, it should be obvious that potatoes will not produce a good crop if your planter is only a few inches deep !

With that in mind, here are a few suggestions for planting vegetables or fruit in the different kind of planters.

Hanging baskets:

Best suited for obvious reasons for short plants such as strawberries, however provided you have not placed the hanger too high, then you could consider using slightly longer chains as suggested earlier, and growing climbing strawberries or vegetables such as peas or beans up the chains.

A hanging basket can also be a good place to plant your lettuce as it is free from the predations of slugs and other ground insects.

Herbs as well grow vigorously in a hanging basket, which is just about the ideal size for a miniature herb garden.

Deep planters:

Deep planters such as the potato planter made from tires or indeed a wooden sided box, suit other things besides potatoes of course. Into this category would come your root vegetables such as carrots, parsnips or sweet potato perhaps.

Other root vegetables such as beetroot, turnip, radish, celeriac etc, can also be grown here of course but strictly speaking can just as easily be grown in a much shallower planter.

Even a decent sized plant-pot as long as it is over say 10 inches deep can be used to grow carrots quite successfully, especially if you raise it up of the ground away from the carrot fly, which tends not to fly over two feet high or so.

Shallow planters:

Anything under say 10 inches would be regarded as a shallow planter. However there is a good selection of vegetables that can be grown in these, the main problem is that the shallower the soil then the harder it is to keep the moisture content just right.

They are much more prone to getting water-logged or drying out very quickly. That said, even an ultra-shallow planter such as the Gutter planter, can grow a selection of herbs for instance such as parsley, mustard , sweet basil, sage thyme etc, and can also be used to bring on seedlings as mentioned earlier.

Wheelbarrow's and other odd-bods:

Containers such as old wheelbarrows and other slightly more ungainly looking planters are ideal for growing climbing plants, such as peas or beans. Training them around the structure not only keeps the vegetable's well ventilated, but also makes something interesting and pleasant to look at.

A climbing strawberry plant such as the Mount Everest climbing strawberry can look quite spectacular, in this situation.

Your own imagination is perhaps the only limit on the kinds of plants you can grow, in the different planters available. Whether you are growing carrots in an old wellington boot, or potatoes in a child's discarded pram; the fact is that there is no end to the containers we can use to plant vegetables that will enhance our larder.

With the present move towards recycling and 'saving the planet' it is suddenly very much in fashion to do something that helps, instead of hinders our move to a safer cleaner environment.

As recycling has grown in popularity, so I am pleased to see is the idea of using material that would often be thrown into the rubbish tip, to produce great healthy vegetables straight from the garden with no "air miles" to count at all, and zero carbon footprint.
I sincerely hope that this work has been of some help to you, and has given you fresh ideas when it comes to planting your vegetables in containers of many kinds.

Renovate old greenhouse?

Oh, and I almost forgot, how to renovate an old greenhouse on a tight budget. For my father it was simple – employ child labour (me) and about 100 square yards of clear plastic to make up for the broken glass on an old Victorian greenhouse.

Job done. The greenhouse grapevine thrived, but the grapes were just what you would expect in Scotland – small and bitter !

Happy planting.

My Notes / To-Do List

Thanks From The Author

Let me just finish by saying a **HUGE THANK YOU** for purchasing my book – it is very much appreciated.

If you have enjoyed it (and hopefully you have!) then I would be delighted if you could take the time to post a quick review on Amazon – you're honest opinion will be much valued by myself and other potential readers.

If you would like more information on the aspects of Raised Bed Gardening as well as other highly effective gardening or Homesteading techniques, then please feel free to check out the following books

***

Relevant Books by Same Author

Raised Bed Gardening 5 Book Bundle

Raised Bed Gardening 3 Book Bundle

Companion Planting

Growing Berries

Square Foot Gardening

Square Foot Vs Raised Bed Gardening

Vegetable Gardening Basics